Published by Creative Education
123 South Broad Street, Mankato, Minnesota 56001
Creative Education is an imprint of The Creative Company

Designed by Stephanie Blumenthal

Photos by: Allsport Photography, Associated Press/Wide World Photos,
Everett Collection, Globe Photos, NBA Photos, Anthony Neste,
Orlando Sentinel, and SportsChrome.

Library of Congress Cataloging-in-Publication Data

Goodman, Michael E.
Shaquille O'Neal / by Michael E. Goodman.
p. cm. — (Ovations)
ISBN 0-88682-633-0

1. O'Neal, Shaquille—Juvenile literature. 2. Basketball players—United States—
Biography—Juvenile literature. [1. O'Neal, Shaquille. 2. Basketball players.
3. Afro-Americans—Biography.]
GV884.054G66 1997   93-49103
796.323'092
[B]—DC20

First edition

5 4 3 2 1

SHAQUILLE

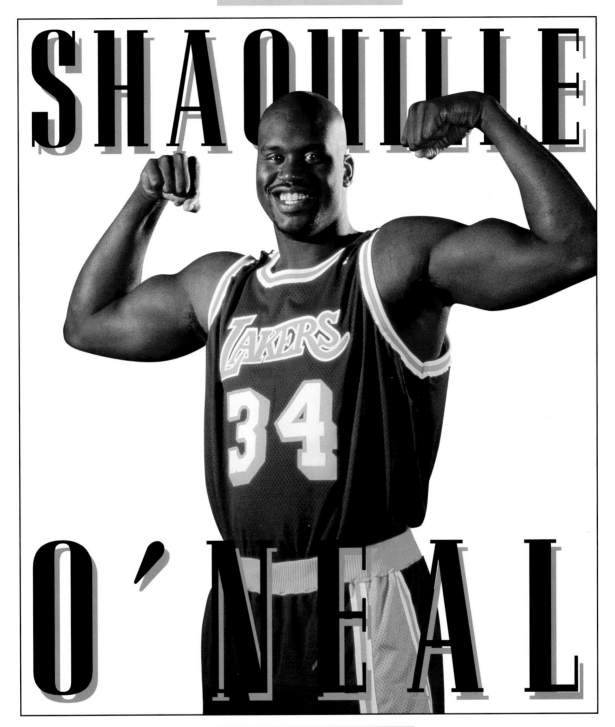

O'NEAL

BY MICHAEL E. GOODMAN

Creative ☾ Education

REFLECTIONS

He's a giant with a shaved head, a warm smile, and awesome power and grace. That's what you notice about Shaquille O'Neal when you see him on the basketball court. Off the court, the smile remains, and his charm and youthful enthusiasm take over. He says he wants to be like Peter Pan and never grow up. "Grown-ups have problems," he says, "and I want to stay happy."

There may never have been an athlete with his combination of size, strength, and personality. He tears down entire backboards one day, and gently comforts a sick child in a hospital ward the next. He once drove 100 miles to pose with a new baby whose parents had named him Shaquille. He makes an incredible

move toward the basket and spectators jump out of their seats. He slams the ball through the hoop and they slap hands. He swats away an opponent's shot and they roar. No one—not the fans in the stands nor the basketball experts—doubts that Shaquille O'Neal has the talent to become an all-time great. Very few athletes command that kind of respect.

All this adoration and interest, however, has left O'Neal with very little peace. Fans wait outside of arenas or hotels just trying to get a glance at him or obtain a prized autograph. Hoping to get him to endorse their products, advertisers flock to his agent, offering unbelievable amounts of money. He has become more than just a person or a basketball player—he's now a corporation with a strong financial bottom line.

Yet what is Shaquille O'Neal really like? He's confident without being brash. He's an "army brat" who moved from base to base so often as a child that he had to become self-reliant. His parents taught him strong personal values, including the importance of leading his own life and not following in someone else's footsteps.

O'Neal has certainly succeeded in creating his own unique path through life—leaving others to follow in the wake of his worldwide fame. He has a licensed trademark, "Shaq Attaq," used as a label on products from sneakers to toys, he has made a top-selling rap recording, starred in Hollywood films and music videos, and found time in his schedule to pick up an Olympic gold medal in 1996 as a member of the U.S. basketball squad known as Dream Team III.

NBA star Shaquille O'Neal has it all: size, strength, and personality. His fans come in all ages. Shaquille starred as a genial genie in the film Kazaam, middle photo. He also starred on the basketball court when he and his teammates won an Olympic gold medal in Atlanta in 1996.

EVOLUTION

Sports fans marvel at the size and power of Shaquille O'Neal. They can't believe that someone so big—he's 7-foot-1, weighs 303 pounds, and wears a size 21EEE shoe—can race down the court so quickly and fluidly. But O'Neal wasn't always comfortable with his size. As a young boy growing up—and up, and up—he found it a challenge to deal with his unique height. Fortunately, he had good parents who were there to help.

Shaquille was born on March 6, 1972, and raised by his mother, Lucille O'Neal. They lived in Newark, New Jersey. When Shaquille was two years old, his mother married Philip Harrison, whom Shaq considers to be his father. Harrison helped raise Shaq from that time on. The couple

decided that the toddler should keep the name "O'Neal" to pass his mother's last name on to another generation. In 1974, Harrison joined the army to do all he could to help the struggling family—which soon included three younger siblings in addition to Shaquille—get ahead financially.

Being in the army meant moving frequently, from state to state and even across the Atlantic Ocean to Germany. Shaquille had to get used to a new elementary school and a new town almost every year. It wasn't always an easy life for the youngster. He was often the new kid in school or on the block, and it was hard to make and keep friends.

Then there was his size. By the time he was 13 years old, Shaquille was already 6-foot-8. His classmates often kidded him, saying that anyone so big must have flunked several times.

His unusual name also led to occasional teasing. Lucille O'Neal Harrison had chosen the name Shaquille Rashaun for her son after studying an Islamic name dictionary. The two words mean "little warrior." "I wanted

Shaquille and his mom share a moment in the kitchen. Lucille Harrison gave unique Islamic names to her four children.

my children to have unique names," she explained. "To me, just having a name that means something makes you special." All of her children received unique Islamic names—Lateefah and Ayesha for Shaquille's younger sisters, Jamal for his younger brother.

Shaquille often became a warrior when someone made fun of his name. He would beat up his tormentors, and then his father would paddle him to keep him in line.

"When I was little, I was kind of a juvenile delinquent, but my father stayed on me," O'Neal said. "Being a drill sergeant, he had to discipline his troops. Then he'd come home and discipline me." Even though Harrison was so strict,

Shaquille O'Neal has been living a basketball player's dream for most of his life. He played in high school and college; he went on to star in the pros, and he even played in the Summer Olympics.

Shaquille developed a very close relationship with him. "My father was tough on me," O'Neal remarked, "because he wanted me to be able to make my own decisions, to do the right thing."

"I told him there's no half-stepping in this life," said Harrison. "He should be a leader, not a follower."

Shaquille took his father's advice and tried to develop talents that would help him find his own unique way in life. Early on, he wanted to be a break dancer. He practiced long hours on various dance moves, including spinning around on his head. Then his body became too wide and long for dancing. When Shaquille turned to basketball, the sport became his obsession.

"I wasn't always blessed with ability," he remembers. "I couldn't dunk until the end of my junior year in high school. When I first started to dunk, I was clumsy

and had bad knees. But I never gave up. When everybody was going to parties and stuff like that, I was outside dribbling, working on my coordination and trying to dunk."

Once, when Shaquille was thirteen, Louisiana State University coach Dale Brown conducted a basketball clinic at the base in Germany where the Harrison family was living. The coach turned to the tall young man near him and asked, "How long have you been in the army?"

When the boy replied that he was just a kid, Brown's eyes immediately lit up. "Uh, can I speak to your father, please?" he asked.

Coach and player both remembered that meeting vividly a few years later, when Brown came to an army base in San Antonio, Texas, to recruit seventeen-year-old Shaquille to play for his LSU squad. O'Neal had just led his Cole High School team to a remarkable 68-1 record over two seasons, including a state championship in his senior year. He was rated as the top

Coach Dale Brown recruited Shaquille to play for LSU. Shaq had led his Cole High School team to a 68-1 record and a Texas state championship.

high school player in the country at the time. During his senior year, he had averaged a remarkable 32.1 points, 22 rebounds, and eight blocked shots per game.

O'Neal agreed to play for Coach Brown at LSU, and, over the next three years, the coach, team, and player went through tumultuous times. LSU had solid winning records all three seasons but never seriously contended for an NCAA title. Shaquille did all that was asked of him. He worked hard on his shooting and defense and exercised for hours every day to increase his physical strength and jumping ability. After much practice, he was able to leap from a standing position and touch a spot more than two feet above the rim.

The hard work paid off. By Shaq's sophomore season, he had broken through as a dominant

college player, averaging nearly 28 points and 15 rebounds per game and ranking among the top shot-blockers. After that sophomore season, O'Neal was chosen to the first team All-America squad and named College Player of the Year.

Unfortunately, Coach Brown was unable to recruit enough other stars to complement his giant in the middle. As a result, opponents were able to focus most of their attention on O'Neal. When Shaq complained about the physical abuse, referees replied that he was so big that he should be able to take it.

The next year, life on the court became almost unbearable for the young star. Opponents triple- and quadruple-teamed him on defense. They also began a dangerous practice of pushing into his legs to throw him off balance

when he went up for dunk attempts. Shaquille O'Neal came to a realization: college basketball had stopped being enjoyable for him. He decided to leave LSU a year early to join the National Basketball Association.

At first, his parents were disappointed. They had hoped their son, who had close to a B average, would finish college and earn his diploma before turning professional. "I told my father I wanted to leave. He just thought about it and finally, he said, 'If I were you, I'd want to leave, too.'"

From the moment that O'Neal announced his intention to enter the 1992 NBA draft, the chase was on to see which team would win the special lottery for first pick. The prize went to the Orlando Magic, one of the NBA's newer and weaker teams.

After three years on the LSU team, Shaq joined the Magic, one of the NBA's newer teams. In the pros, Shaq muscled his way around the opposition and towered over players like Spud Webb, top photo.

Orlando selected Shaquille and then pursued the difficult task of signing him to a contract. Magic general manager Pat Williams had to do a lot of wheeling and dealing to lower the team's total pay in order to fit a big contract for O'Neal under the league salary limit. Finally, the details were worked out. Shaquille signed for $40 million over seven years, becoming the highest-paid performer in the league even before he played his first NBA game. The money didn't change Shaquille from being a fun-loving 20-year-old, however. The night he signed the big contract, he headed back to San Antonio and treated several friends to a night at a water-slide park.

Shaquille also attracted the interest of many advertisers. A shoe company agreed to pay him $10 million over five years to wear its new "Shaq Sneakers," a toy company created a Shaq action figure, a clothing company designed a line of sportswear bearing his name, and a sporting goods firm began marketing a "Shaq Attaq" basketball.

Shaq and Horace Grant played together in Orlando. Shaq became the first rookie to start in the NBA's All-Star Game since Michael Jordan in 1985.

Shaquille was now a multinational corporation and a multimillionaire. But could he live up to his reputation on the court, competing against the best players in the world? He answered that one quickly. One after another, the new NBA star took on the league's best big men—Hakeem Olajuwon, Patrick Ewing, Robert Parish, David Robinson. Sometimes they outshined him. But more and more often he held his own—and sometimes even outscored them. There were definite weaknesses in O'Neal's game—he was a poor free-throw shooter, picked up unnecessary fouls, and was inconsistent with his jump shot. But he still became the first rookie to start in the NBA's All-Star Game since Michael Jordan in 1985. He also helped turn the Magic from one of the worst teams in the league into a solid contender.

In 1992-93, the Magic nearly made the playoffs for the first time. Shaquille easily earned the league's Rookie of the Year honor, ranking number two in the NBA in rebounding, number three in shooting percentage, and number eight in scoring.

During his second year, Shaq was second in the league in both scoring and rebounding, and the Magic did indeed reach the playoffs. And year three was even better. O'Neal topped the league in scoring, while the Magic roared past Michael Jordan's Chicago Bulls and then the Indiana Pacers to reach the NBA Finals. No team in NBA history had ever reached the finals in only six years. The Magic were contenders, but they didn't become champions. They lost four straight games to the Houston Rockets for the league title. The Magic fell short again in 1995-96, bowing to the Bulls in the Eastern Conference finals and leaving Shaq and his teammates still without championship rings.

Shaquille was named the NBA's Rookie of the Year in 1993. His energy and drive brought the Magic closer to a championship than they had ever been before.

Though the season ended on a losing note, O'Neal became a big winner financially a few months later. An escape clause in his original contract with the Magic enabled Shaq to become a free agent after four seasons in Orlando. While he enjoyed playing in Florida, Shaq had always wanted to play in Los Angeles for the Lakers. The Lakers had a long winning tradition, and Los Angeles, with Hollywood nearby, seemed the perfect place for a showman like Shaq. The Lakers and Magic both offered huge contracts to the young

center—more than $115 million for seven years. No matter which team he picked, Shaq would be signing the largest sports contract of all time. After thinking over the matter for several weeks, he chose to follow his dream to the West Coast.

Shaq told reporters that his decision to change clubs wasn't made just for money or because he thought he could win a championship more quickly with the Lakers than the Magic. Most importantly, he felt that Los Angeles was a place that fit his personality better than Orlando and offered him greater opportunity to pursue his interests off the court as well as on it.

It is hard to imagine how Shaq can be more successful in his off-court pursuits. His

commercials for sneakers, soft drinks, and food products have filled television screens around the world, and he has already starred on the big screen as a sensitive basketball player in the film *Blue Chips* and as a genial genie in *Kazaam*. Shaq has even fulfilled a special ambition by making a rap album, *Shaq Diesel*, which has sold more than one million copies. He followed that with *Shaq Fu: Da Return*.

Fame and fortune, however, has had its price. Shaquille can no longer walk comfortably in public or go to a restaurant or a store without being surrounded by adoring fans who want to touch him or get his autograph. His height makes it almost impossible for him to hide, even in a big crowd. The Orlando Magic team bus had to drive inside an arena to let off the players in order to avoid the crush of fans who wanted to see "the Shaq." Despite all of the pressures, Shaquille has been generous about sharing his money and his time with the needy and sick. He regularly visits children's wards in hospitals and does not seek publicity about his activities. He has

Shaq signed autographs during a tour before the Olympics in 1996. He also changed teams in 1996, moving from Orlando to Los Angeles.

sponsored several "Shaqsgiving" celebrations, supplying Thanksgiving dinner for homeless people in Orlando and even working in the food line himself. Sensitive about dropping out of college, Shaq has made commercials and speeches urging youngsters to stay in school.

O'Neal's talent and personality have earned him a special place in the hearts of sports fans everywhere. What is his reaction to all of the publicity and adoration? He takes it in stride. When asked to describe himself recently, he said, "Shaquille O'Neal is a basketball player, slash, entertainer, slash, young guy, slash, funny, likable guy." For someone headed for the top of the sports and advertising worlds, he certainly seems to have his values well grounded.

Shaq is a singing star as well as an athlete. His first rap album has sold more than one million copies. He also represented the U.S. at the 1996 Summer Olympics along with gold-medal-winning gymnast Dominique Moceanu, middle photo.

VOICES

ON HIS UPBRINGING AND FAMILY:

"The worst part was traveling. Meeting people, getting tight with them, and then having to leave. Sometimes you come into a new place, and they'll test you. Teased about my name. Teased about my size. Teased about being flunked. You know, 'You're so big, you must have flunked.' I'd have to beat them up. It took a while to gain friends because people thought I was mean. I had a bad temper."

Shaquille O'Neal

"His father was then, and still is, the buzz in the boy's conscience, a hovering reminder of what is expected of an honest man, a man others assemble behind to follow."

Mick Elliott, sportswriter

"Shaq says he will get his degree later, and what he says he'll do, he usually does. But I know that later has never come for me. When I got out of high school, I told myself I would go to college, but I got married young and I chose to stay home with the children. I enjoyed that, but I always regretted not getting that college degree. I know there's all that money out there, but I want him to have that diploma, so he'll have something to depend on."

Lucille Harrison,
Shaquille's mother

"It takes a lot to get me excited. You know what gets me excited? When my mom tells me she loves me. That's the only thing I can think of."

Shaquille O'Neal

"My dream is to have six boys so I can have six branches of O'Neals. I'm going to care for their needs, make them smile, make them laugh."

Shaquille O'Neal

ON BEING A CELEBRITY:

"Most of the time there are a couple of hundred fans waiting for us, outside the arena, at the hotel, anywhere they think they might see Shaq. This has gone way beyond basketball. It must be what it was like to have traveled with the Beatles."

Alex Martins,
public relations director
for the Orlando Magic

"Let's say I'm at an airport, and I'm buying some mints in the gift shop. There might be somebody there trying to figure out who I am, but that only lasts a second. I mean, they are standing right at the magazine rack, and I'm on the cover of about four of them."

Shaquille O'Neal

"We want to portray him as the strongest man in the NBA, and we want to do it worldwide. We're going to put him in fifty countries."

Mark D. Holtzman,
director of marketing for Reebok

Shaquille says that he left Orlando for L.A. because he wanted to pursue his interests off the court, one of which is movie acting. The role of the genie in Kazaam, top photo, presented a kind of new challenge that Shaq now enjoys.

"Basketball is really the main thing. If it wasn't for basketball, none of the other doors would be open for me. In order to do those other things, I must stay on top of my game. If I did all those other things first, then I would slack off my game a little bit. And that's not going to happen."

Shaquille O'Neal

ON HIS PERSONALITY:

"He's a combination of the Terminator and Bambi. That's very rare."

Leonard Armato, O'Neal's agent

"Ego is acting like you're all-that. Like they say on the block, 'all-that.' Can't anybody touch you. Confidence is knowing who you are."

Shaquille O'Neal

"He's very humble. He's not a loud-mouth, and he has good human skills. He fits in and doesn't put himself on a pedestal."

Pat Williams,
Orlando Magic
executive vice president

ON HIS PLAYING ABILITY:

"I'm happy the fans like to see me play. I'm 7-foot-1, 300 pounds. I can dunk hard. I slide on the floor. I get rebounds. I can dribble the length of the floor. People like to see that. If I was a fan, I'd want to see Shaq play, too."

Shaquille O'Neal

"Shaquille has that quick, unrestrainable explosion, like Charles Barkley. It's a raw power you don't get in the weight room. It comes from somewhere else, deep in the soul. This guy may have the talent and discipline to be the best."

Bill Walton,
television analyst and
former star NBA center

As Dream Team III at the 1996 Summer Olympics, Shaq and his teammates played hard and put on a spectacular show, running away with the gold medal.

"He brings a new dimension to the game. He is electrifying, he's a tremendous shot-blocker, and he's extremely graceful and fluid. He's also got the power—it's already terrifying—and everyone is going to play him for his power. The league is full of 300-pound guys who will be glad to butt heads with him, like two bull elephants, and it's going to wear him down. He's got to learn to score without going inside all the time."

Wilt Chamberlain,
NBA Hall of Fame center

"He's got the physical and mental gifts to be as good as Chamberlain and Jabbar, but you're talking a bunch of MVP awards, championship trophies, and Hall of Fame. That's a long way down the road. But as far as physique, the athleticism, the mental makeup, the balance of his life—it's all there. Shaq can go to any level that he wants to. I think he wants to be good."

Pat Williams,
Orlando Magic
executive vice president

"Don't call Shaquille the next anybody. Let him be the first Shaquille."

Kareem Abdul-Jabbar,
former star NBA center

In 1996, after only four years in the league, Shaquille O'Neal was named one of the 50 greatest players in NBA history. Also named were Robert Parish, top, and Kareem Abdul-Jabbar, bottom photo. The list was compiled to celebrate the NBA's 50th anniversary.

ON HIS BASKETBALL AMBITION:

"I've got ten fingers and no rings. And I love jewelry."

Shaquille O'Neal,
from one of his commercials

ON HIS FUTURE DEVELOPMENT:

"I'm smarter. I have a few more moves down low, and I'm stronger and quicker. Every year I've tried to get better at certain things. Now all I have to do is hit my free throws and I'll be unstoppable."

Shaquille O'Neal

On the relationship of basketball and his Hollywood acting career:

"Everybody in the NBA is an actor, anyway. They give each other bad looks and complain to the refs."

Shaquille O'Neal

On his team, the Los Angeles Lakers:

"The era of 'Magic' Johnson and 'Show Time' was a great era for the Lakers. Now it's time to start a new era with Shaq."

Del Harris, Lakers coach

Off the court, Shaq stars in music videos, movies, and commercials. On the court, number 34 Shaquille O'Neal is ushering in a bold new era for the Los Angeles Lakers.

OVATIONS